History's Famous Friendships

SUSAN B. ANTHONY AND ELIZABETH CADY STANTON

By Shannon H. Harts

Gareth Stevens PUBLISHING

Please visit our website, www.garethstevens.com. For a free color catalog of all our high-quality books, call toll free 1-800-542-2595 or fax 1-877-542-2596.

Library of Congress Cataloging-in-Publication Data

Names: Harts, Shannon H., author.
Title: Susan B. Anthony and Elizabeth Cady Stanton / Shannon H. Harts.
Description: New York : Gareth Stevens Publishing, [2022] | Series: History's famous friendships | Includes index.
Identifiers: LCCN 2020038071 (print) | LCCN 2020038072 (ebook) | ISBN 9781538265079 (library binding) | ISBN 9781538265055 (paperback) | ISBN 9781538265062 (set) | ISBN 9781538265086 (ebook)
Subjects: LCSH: Women's rights--United States--Juvenile literature. | Women--Suffrage--United States--Juvenile literature. | Anthony, Susan B. (Susan Brownell), 1820-1906. | Stanton, Elizabeth Cady, 1815-1902.
Classification: LCC HQ1236.5.U5 H38 2022 (print) | LCC HQ1236.5.U5 (ebook) | DDC 305.42092/273--dc23
LC record available at https://lccn.loc.gov/2020038071
LC ebook record available at https://lccn.loc.gov/2020038072

First Edition

Published in 2022 by
Gareth Stevens Publishing
111 East 14th Street, Suite 349
New York, NY 10003

Designer: Katelyn E. Reynolds
Editor: Therese Shea

Photo credits: Cvr, pp. 1 (Anthony), 5, 7, 11, 16, 17, 21, 23, 25, 26, 28, 29 courtesy of the Library of Congress; cvr, p. 1 (Stanton) National Portrait Gallery, Smithsonian Institution; cvr, pp. 1-32 (background) wawritto/Shutterstock.com; pp. 1-32 (frame) Olesia Misty/Shutterstock.com; cvr, pp. 1-32 (border) Vasya Kobelev/Shutterstock.com; p. 7 http://digital.library.upenn.edu/women/stanton/years/years.html/Binksternet/Wikipedia.org; p. 8 Universal History Archive/Universal Images Group via Getty Images; p. 9 Interim Archives/Getty Images; pp. 11, 13, 14 Bettmann/Getty Images; p. 12 MPI/Getty Images; p. 15 Dennis Macdonald/Photolibrary/Getty Images Plus; p. 16 Ken Florey Suffrage Collection/Gado/Getty Images; p. 19 courtesy of the National Archives and Recoreds Administration; p. 19 Time Life Pictures/Mansell/The LIFE Picture Collection via Getty Images; p. 27 Library of Congress/Corbis/VCG via Getty Images.

Printed in the United States of America

CPSIA compliance information: Batch #CSGS22: For further information contact Gareth Stevens, New York, New York at 1-800-542-2595.

CONTENTS

*Words in the Glossary appear in **bold** type the first time they are used in the text.*

PASSIONATE ABOUT MORE POWER

In the mid-1800s, American women lacked many rights. Most couldn't own property or vote. They had fewer job opportunities and earned less money than men. They didn't have a voice in **politics** in order to make changes.

In 1851, a woman named Elizabeth Cady Stanton met a former teacher named Susan B. Anthony in New York. Before long, they had a strong friendship. They also had a powerful partnership in the fight for women's suffrage, or the right to vote.

MORE TO KNOW

ANTHONY AND STANTON FOUGHT FOR THE RIGHT TO VOTE IN MANY WAYS. THEY TALKED TO MEMBERS OF THE U.S. GOVERNMENT, GAVE SPEECHES, AND WROTE ABOUT THEIR IDEAS IN NEWSPAPERS.

Stanton and Anthony brought out the best in each other as they worked to give women more power over their lives.

LEARNING THE LAW

On November 12, 1815, Elizabeth Cady was born in Johnstown, New York. As a girl, she sometimes studied in the law office of her father, Daniel Cady. She learned how women and men weren't equal under the law.

After her older brother, Eleazar, died, there were no boys left in the family. Elizabeth tried to comfort her father. He said, "Oh my daughter, I wish you were a boy!" Stanton said these words made her work even harder to be seen as equal to any man.

MORE TO KNOW

AFTER ELIZABETH AND HENRY STANTON WERE MARRIED IN 1840, THEY TRAVELED TO THE WORLD ANTI-SLAVERY **CONVENTION** IN LONDON, ENGLAND. WOMEN COULDN'T TAKE PART, HOWEVER.

Henry Brewster Stanton

Although Elizabeth's father didn't approve, she married **abolitionist** speaker and lawyer Henry Brewster Stanton in 1840. They had seven children, including her daughter Harriot, shown above.

EARLY BELIEF IN EQUALITY

On February 15, 1820, Susan Brownell Anthony was born in Adams, Massachusetts. Her parents, Daniel and Lucy, raised her to follow the Quaker faith. This included a belief that everyone is equal under God.

Anthony showed her intelligence from a young age. She could read and write when she was 3. After completing her schooling, she worked as a teacher for about 10 years. Then she decided to move to her family's home near Rochester, New York. There, she met leaders of the abolitionist movement.

Susan B. Anthony

In 1849, Anthony moved to Gates, west of Rochester, to manage the family farm. She later lived in Rochester, where her home (above) is open to visitors today.

MORE TO KNOW

WHEN SHE WAS AROUND 16, ANTHONY BEGAN TO PASS AROUND ANTISLAVERY **PETITIONS**. SHE ONCE SAID, "TRUST ME THAT AS I **IGNORE** ALL LAW TO HELP THE SLAVE, SO WILL I IGNORE IT ALL TO PROTECT AN **ENSLAVED** WOMAN."

CREATING THE CONVENTION

Elizabeth Cady Stanton first met Lucretia Mott at the World Anti-Slavery Convention in 1840. On July 13, 1848, Stanton had tea with Mott and others in Waterloo, New York. They organized, or planned, an event that had never happened before in the United States: a convention for women's rights.

They decided to hold the convention in Seneca Falls, New York, on July 19 and 20, 1848. Although Anthony didn't attend, this convention began the women's rights movement that Anthony and Stanton would lead.

MORE TO KNOW

AT THE SENECA FALLS CONVENTION, STANTON READ THE DECLARATION OF SENTIMENTS. SHE MODELED IT AFTER THE DECLARATION OF INDEPENDENCE, THE PIECE OF WRITING IN WHICH THE AMERICAN COLONIES SAID THEY WERE FREE FROM BRITISH RULE.

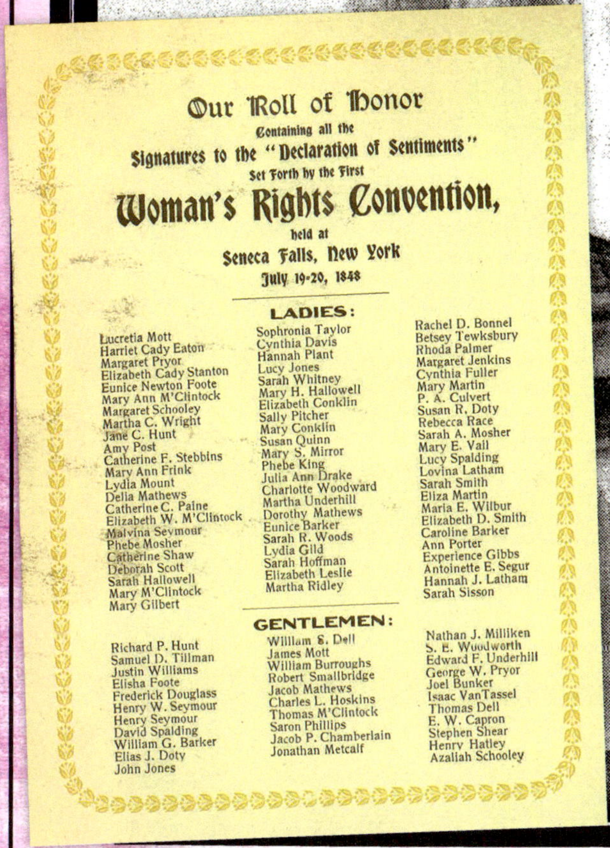

Our Roll of Honor

Containing all the

Signatures to the "Declaration of Sentiments"

Set Forth by the First

Woman's Rights Convention,

held at

Seneca Falls, New York

July 19-20, 1848

LADIES:

Lucretia Mott
Harriet Cady Eaton
Margaret Pryor
Elizabeth Cady Stanton
Eunice Newton Foote
Mary Ann M'Clintock
Margaret Schooley
Martha C. Wright
Jane C. Hunt
Amy Post
Catherine F. Stebbins
Mary Ann Frink
Lydia Mount
Delia Mathews
Catherine C. Paine
Elizabeth W. M'Clintock
Malvina Seymour
Phebe Mosher
Catherine Shaw
Deborah Scott
Sarah Hallowell
Mary M'Clintock
Mary Gilbert

Sophronia Taylor
Cynthia Davis
Hannah Plant
Lucy Jones
Sarah Whitney
Mary H. Hallowell
Elizabeth Conklin
Sally Pitcher
Mary Conklin
Susan Quinn
Mary S. Mirror
Phebe King
Julia Ann Drake
Charlotte Woodward
Martha Underhill
Dorothy Mathews
Eunice Barker
Sarah R. Woods
Lydia Gild
Sarah Hoffman
Elizabeth Leslie
Martha Ridley

Rachel D. Bonnel
Betsey Tewksbury
Rhoda Palmer
Margaret Jenkins
Cynthia Fuller
Mary Martin
P. A. Culvert
Susan R. Doty
Rebecca Race
Sarah A. Mosher
Mary E. Vail
Lucy Spalding
Lovina Latham
Sarah Smith
Eliza Martin
Maria E. Wilbur
Elizabeth D. Smith
Caroline Barker
Ann Porter
Experience Gibbs
Antoinette E. Segur
Hannah J. Latham
Sarah Sisson

GENTLEMEN:

Richard P. Hunt
Samuel D. Tillman
Justin Williams
Elisha Foote
Frederick Douglass
Henry W. Seymour
Henry Seymour
David Spalding
William G. Barker
Elias J. Doty
John Jones

William S. Dell
James Mott
William Burroughs
Robert Smallbridge
Jacob Mathews
Charles L. Hoskins
Thomas M'Clintock
Saron Phillips
Jacob P. Chamberlain
Jonathan Metcalf

Nathan J. Milliken
S. E. Woodworth
Edward F. Underhill
George W. Pryor
Joel Bunker
Isaac VanTassel
Thomas Dell
E. W. Capron
Stephen Shear
Henry Hatley
Azaliah Schooley

The Declaration of Sentiments used words from the Declaration of Independence but added "woman" and "women." For example, the Declaration of Sentiments stated: "We hold these truths to be self-evident [clear] that all men and women are created equal."

Lucretia Mott

THE RISE OF AN ORGANIZER

At the time of the Seneca Falls Convention, Susan B. Anthony was a temperance worker. This meant she worked to limit people's use of **alcohol**. Since drinking often led men to mistreat women, Anthony thought this could help women.

However, at a New York State convention for temperance, she was stopped from speaking. She was told, "The ladies have been invited to listen and learn and not to speak." Events such as this made Anthony more interested in working for women's rights.

temperance workers pray outside a New York bar

MORE TO KNOW

IN 1852, SUSAN B. ANTHONY ATTENDED HER FIRST WOMEN'S RIGHTS CONVENTION. THE SAME YEAR, STANTON AND ANTHONY HELPED FORM THE WOMEN'S NEW YORK STATE TEMPERANCE SOCIETY.

In 1848, Anthony gave her first public speech. A talented speaker, she later delivered as many as 100 speeches a year.

A FRIENDSHIP FORMS IN SENECA FALLS

On the evening of May 12, 1851, Anthony and Stanton's life-changing first meeting took place on a Seneca Falls street corner. They had just attended an antislavery meeting led by abolitionists William Lloyd Garrison and George Thompson.

Anthony had been staying at the home of her friend Amelia Bloomer. Bloomer **introduced** the two women. Stanton later said of Anthony: "I liked her thoroughly, and why I did not at once invite her home with me to dinner, I do not know."

A monument in Seneca Falls, New York, shows what the meeting between Anthony, left, and Stanton, right, may have looked like. Amelia Bloomer, center, was a friend to both.

MORE TO KNOW

STANTON AND ANTHONY WERE IN THEIR 30s WHEN THEY MET. STANTON HAD CHILDREN WHILE ANTHONY DIDN'T. ANTHONY BABYSAT STANTON'S CHILDREN AT TIMES WHEN STANTON NEEDED TO WORK FOR THEIR COMMON CAUSES.

A POWERFUL PARTNERSHIP

Susan B. Anthony respected Elizabeth Cady Stanton's ideas and writing skills. Stanton recognized Anthony's speaking skills and ability to organize. They became a powerful force for the many causes they cared about.

From 1861 to 1865, the Union (the Northern states) and the Confederacy (the Southern states) fought the American Civil War. Anthony and Stanton formed the Women's Loyal National League. They called for freeing all enslaved people and granting them the rights of U.S. citizens.

The Women's Loyal National League raised money to help Harriet Tubman, shown here. Tubman was a formerly enslaved woman who helped others escape slavery. She became a Union spy too.

MORE TO KNOW

IN 1864, STANTON AND ANTHONY ASKED AMERICAN WOMEN TO SIGN A PETITION TO END SLAVERY. "WHILE SLAVERY EXISTS ANYWHERE THERE CAN BE FREEDOM NOWHERE," THEIR MESSAGE READ.

POST-WAR PETITION

After the Civil War, Congress had the task of including the rights of Black Americans in the Constitution, the highest law in the nation. Stanton and Anthony saw this as a chance for women to be given more rights too.

On January 29, 1866, they presented a petition to Congress for "universal suffrage." This meant that all adult U.S. citizens could vote. However, the petition was unsuccessful. Stanton and Anthony spent the rest of their lives preparing the way for women to win suffrage from the federal, or national, government.

MORE TO KNOW

THE FOURTEENTH **AMENDMENT** TO THE CONSTITUTION GAVE FORMERLY ENSLAVED PEOPLE CITIZENSHIP. THE FIFTEENTH AMENDMENT MADE IT CLEAR THAT THE RIGHT TO VOTE WAS ONLY FOR BLACK MEN, THOUGH.

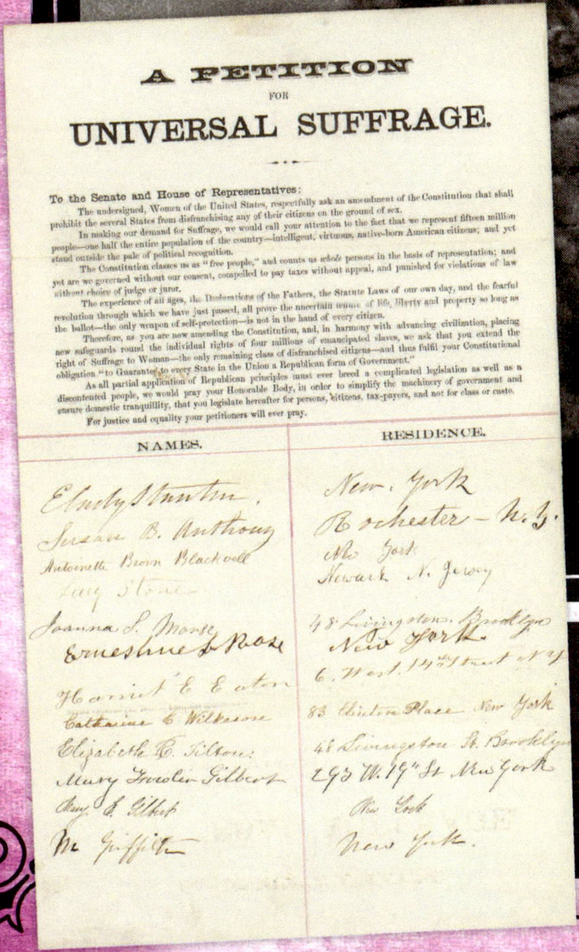

A PETITION

FOR

UNIVERSAL SUFFRAGE.

To the Senate and House of Representatives:

The undersigned, Women of the United States, respectfully ask an amendment of the Constitution that shall prohibit the several States from disfranchising any of their citizens on the ground of sex.

In making our demand for Suffrage, we would call your attention to the fact that we represent fifteen million people—one half the entire population of the country—intelligent, virtuous, native-born American citizens; and yet stand outside the pale of political recognition.

The Constitution classes us as "free people," and counts us *whole* persons in the basis of representation; and yet are we governed without our consent, compelled to pay taxes without appeal, and punished for violations of law without choice of judge or juror.

The experience of all ages, the Declarations of the Fathers, the Statute Laws of our own day, and the fearful revolution through which we have just passed, all prove the uncertain tenure of life, liberty and property so long as the ballot—the only weapon of self-protection—is not in the hand of every citizen.

Therefore, as you are now amending the Constitution, and, in harmony with advancing civilization, placing new safeguards round the individual rights of four millions of emancipated slaves, we ask that you extend the right of Suffrage to Woman—the only remaining class of disfranchised citizens—and thus fulfil your Constitutional obligation "to Guarantee to every State in the Union a Republican form of Government."

As all partial application of Republican principles must ever breed a complicated legislation as well as a discontented people, we would pray your Honorable Body, in order to simplify the machinery of government and ensure domestic tranquillity, that you legislate hereafter for persons, citizens, tax-payers, and not for class or caste.

For justice and equality your petitioners will ever pray.

NAMES.	RESIDENCE.
E. Cady Stanton	New York
Susan B. Anthony	Rochester – N.Y.
Antoinette Brown Blackwell	New York
Lucy Stone	Newark N. Jersey
Joanna S. Morse	48 Livingston St. Brooklyn
Ernestine L. Rose	New York
Harriet E. Eaton	6 West 14th Street N.Y.
Catharine C. Wilkeson	83 Clinton Place New York
Elizabeth R. Tilton	48 Livingston St. Brooklyn
Mary Fowler Gilbert	293 W. 19th St New York
[illegible]	New York
[illegible]	New York

In 1866, Stanton became the first woman to run for the U.S. **House of Representatives**. She didn't win, but she and Anthony didn't give up their efforts to change the law.

REVOLUTIONARY WRITING

Anthony and Stanton needed to gain more support for women's suffrage. They formed a weekly women's rights newspaper called the *Revolution*. Its first issue ran on January 8, 1868.

The *Revolution* began less than three years after the Civil War. Black Americans were still working for the right to vote. Some women thought that they should focus on the right to vote for Black men before the right to vote for women. Some of these women belonged to the American Woman Suffrage Association (AWSA).

MORE TO KNOW

SUSAN B. ANTHONY WAS THE PROPRIETOR, OR OWNER, OF THE *REVOLUTION*. STANTON AND THE ABOLITIONIST PARKER PILLSBURY WERE EDITORS.

The Revolution.

PRINCIPLE, NOT POLICY: JUSTICE, NOT FAVORS.

VOL. I.—NO. 1. NEW YORK, WEDNESDAY, JANUARY 8, 1868. $2.00 A YEAR.

The Revolution;

THE ORGAN OF THE

NATIONAL PARTY OF NEW AMERICA.

KANSAS.

THE BALLOT—BREAD, VIRTUE, POWER.

ELIZABETH CADY STANTON,
PARKER PILLSBURY, Eds.

SUSAN B. ANTHONY,
Proprietor and Manager.

The first issue of the *Revolution* is shown at left. Around 3,000 people received the newspaper at one point. It became an important voice in the women's rights movement.

FEARLESSLY FIGHTING FOR SUFFRAGE

In 1869, Anthony and Stanton took another bold step. They formed the National Woman Suffrage Association (NWSA). This group worked to make Congress pass an amendment that would allow women to vote. It also addressed other rights for women connected to marriage and **divorce**.

In 1890, the NWSA joined forces with the American Woman Suffrage Association. Together, they became the National American Woman Suffrage Association (NAWSA). Stanton was its first president until 1892. Then Anthony became president until 1900.

MORE TO KNOW

THE AWSA BACKED THE FIFTEENTH AMENDMENT AS IT WAS, GIVING BLACK MEN THE RIGHT TO VOTE. THE NWSA WAS AGAINST IT UNLESS IT INCLUDED WOMEN.

By 1910, the NAWSA had about 117,000 members.

ANTHONY'S ARREST

On November 5, 1872, Susan B. Anthony and several other women voted in Rochester, New York, in the presidential election. Two weeks later, the women were arrested for voting illegally.

Anthony didn't want to pay bail. Bail is the money given to a court that allows a prisoner to leave jail until their court date. She had learned that if she went to jail, she could try to prove her case in federal courts. However, Anthony's lawyer paid for her bail because he didn't want her in jail.

MORE TO KNOW

ANTHONY'S **TRIAL** WAS IN A COURT IN CANANDAIGUA, NEW YORK. ANGERING MANY, THE JUDGE ORDERED THE **JURY** TO FIND HER GUILTY AND MAKE HER PAY A $100 FINE.

After voting, Anthony wrote in a letter to Stanton, "Well I have . . . done it!!" After her trial, she never paid the fine.

MAKING PROGRESS

Susan B. Anthony was seen as a hero after her trial. She had been willing to spend time in jail for the right to vote. Her arrest made some people in government think again about the need for an amendment for women's suffrage.

In 1878, Senator Aaron A. Sargent introduced a sixteenth amendment to Congress. This came to be called the Anthony Amendment. It would have given women the right to vote. However, the Senate didn't pass it. Still, Anthony and Stanton wouldn't give up.

Senator Aaron A. Sargent

In 1888, Stanton and Anthony formed the International Council of Women in Washington, DC. It took their concern for women's rights worldwide.

THEIR LASTING LEGACY

In 1895, Stanton and other women published a book called *The Woman's Bible*. Anthony didn't fully agree with the book, but she and Stanton remained friends. They worked on writing several volumes of the *History of Woman Suffrage*. These books recorded the work of many people in the fight for women's rights.

Stanton died in 1902, and Anthony died in 1906, both at age 86. They didn't live to see women gain the right to vote in 1920 through the Nineteenth Amendment. However, their teamwork had made it possible.

signing of the Nineteenth Amendment in Missouri

Stanton and Anthony's Fight for Suffrage

1851
Anthony and Stanton meet in Seneca Falls, New York, where Stanton had organized the Seneca Falls Convention three years before.

1864
Anthony and Stanton call on women to sign a petition against slavery.

1866
Anthony and Stanton ask Congress to include universal suffrage in the Constitution.

1866
Stanton is the first woman to run for the U.S. House of Representatives.

1868
Anthony and Stanton begin the *Revolution* newspaper.

1869
Anthony and Stanton create the National Woman Suffrage Association.

1872
Anthony is arrested for voting in the presidential election and later found guilty.

1881
The first volume of the *History of Woman Suffrage* is published.

1888
The International Council of Women is formed.

1902
Stanton dies.

1906
Anthony dies.

1920
The Nineteenth Amendment gives women the right to vote.

GLOSSARY

abolitionist: one who fights to end slavery

alcohol: a clear liquid with a strong smell that is found in drinks such as beer and wine and that can have an effect on people's actions

amendment: a change or addition to a constitution

convention: a gathering of people who have a common interest or purpose

divorce: the ending of a marriage

enslaved: being "owned" by another person and forced to work without pay

House of Representatives: one part of Congress, which is the branch of the U.S. government that makes laws

ignore: to refuse to show that you heard or saw something

introduce: to make someone known to another person by name. Also, to present something to be considered and discussed, often by a group.

jury: a group of people who are chosen to make a decision in a court case

petition: a written request signed by many people asking the government to take an action

politics: the activities of the government and government officials

trial: a meeting in a court in which evidence about crimes, disagreements, or other events is presented to a judge and often a jury so that legal decisions can be made

For More Information

Books

Cipriano, Jeri. *Elizabeth Cady Stanton: Fighter for Women's Rights*. Egremont, MA: Red Chair Press, 2020

Fankhouser, Kris. *Susan B. Anthony*. Chicago, IL: World Book, Inc., 2018.

Harris, Duchess. *Women's Suffrage*. Minneapolis, MN: Abdo Publishing, 2018.

Websites

Coloring Page: Susan B. Anthony House
www.nps.gov/articles/susan-b-anthony-house-coloring-page.htm
Check out a creative way to learn more about Susan B. Anthony.

Women's Suffrage
www.ducksters.com/history/civil_rights/womens_suffrage.php
Find out more about Anthony and Stanton's roles with the women's suffrage movement.

Publisher's note to educators and parents: Our editors have carefully reviewed these websites to ensure that they are suitable for students. Many websites change frequently, however, and we cannot guarantee that a site's future contents will continue to meet our high standards of quality and educational value. Be advised that students should be closely supervised whenever they access the internet.

INDEX